LITTLE BIG BOOKS

PREHISTORIC ANIMALS

KENNETH LOWTHER

Editor: Trisha Pike   Designer: Jacky Cowdrey
Picture Researcher: Kathy Brandt

Purnell

Above: Digging for fossils has to be done very carefully.

1 FOSSILS' SECRETS

Many millions of years ago forests and swamps covered the Earth. These places were very warm and wet and full of many different kinds of plants and animals. Most of the strange animals that lived millions of years ago have died out. We do not know why they disappeared.

Today people find out about these very early times by studying fossils. Fossils are early plants or the bones and shells of animals that lived on our Earth long ago. They are usually found in rock or ice.

Above: Skeletons of early animals in a museum.

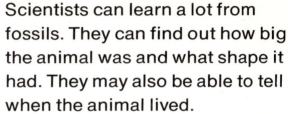

Scientists can learn a lot from fossils. They can find out how big the animal was and what shape it had. They may also be able to tell when the animal lived.

Most fossils are quite small. They may be just tiny pieces of bone or a tooth. A scientist may be lucky and find that he has a whole skeleton. You can see skeletons of prehistoric animals in natural history museums.

Nearly everything we know about these early animals comes from fossils. Scientists are always hoping to find new ones. Gaps in the story of the past may then be filled.

Left: Scientists can find out what animals long ago looked like by studying fossils.

2 LIFE BEGINS

Life first began about 600 million years ago. We do not know exactly how it started. But we do know that very small animals lived in the sea by that time. These animals had no backbones. They were like modern jellyfish, sponges and worms.

Many of the earliest animals were trilobites. These were shellfish with jointed legs. Trilobites were quite lively. Some other kinds of early shellfish hardly moved at all. For example, most of the brachiopods, or lamp-shells, fixed themselves to the sandy sea-bed.

Below left: Life during the Cambrian period:
1. Jellyfish.
2. Sponges.
3. Brachiopods.
4. Trilobites.

Left: Fossil trilobites. They lived on the sea-bed long ago.

Over millions of years many new kinds of animals gradually appeared in the seas. One kind are called nautiloids. They were large shellfish. Some had straight shells while others were curved or bent. There were also fierce-looking animals called eurypterids which were three metres long and looked like scorpions do today.

The animals without backbones were the only form of life for millions of years. But very slowly the first animals with backbones appeared.

**Below right:
The seas in
Silurian times:
1. Brachiopods.
2. Nautiloids.
3. Eurypterid.
4. Worm.**

3 FIRST ANCESTORS

Very, very gradually some of these early animals grew backbones. This is the sort of change which we call evolution. We ourselves are animals with backbones so these fish were our first ancestors.

The first animals with backbones were small fish called ostracoderms. They had large, flat bony heads. Instead of jaws, they had little holes for mouths. They had heavy bodies covered with plates of bony armour. At first they lived in lakes and rivers. Later they spread to the seas.

Above: Three kinds of ostracoderms:
1. Drepanaspis.
2. Pteraspis.
3. Hemicyclaspis.

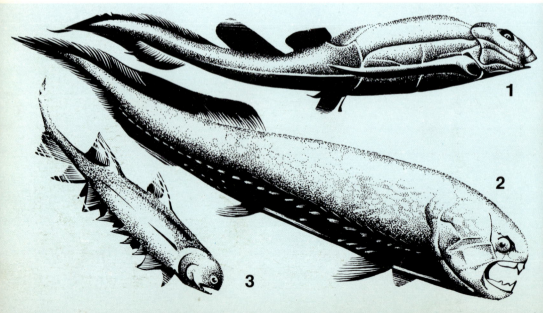

By the time the first bony fish had arrived in the seas new types of fish with jaws had also appeared. The earliest fish with jaws are called placoderms. There were three kinds of placoderms—the antiarchs, the arthrodires and the acanthodians. The antiarchs, such as Bothriolepis, were small fish. They had short tails, flat heads and their bodies were covered in thick bone.

The fierce arthrodires lived at the same time. They had bony plates only on their heads and long flexible tails for swimming fast. The acanthodians lived much longer than the antiarchs or the arthrodires. They did not have bony plates, but had spines and scales instead.

Left: The first fish with jaws were the placoderms:
1. Antiarch.
2. Arthrodire.
3. Acanthodian.

Right: The fossil head of Bothriolepis, a small fish.

4 THE LOBE FINS

Above: Early dragonflies looked very like dragonflies of today.

Fish in the water breathe in oxygen through gills. But the water some of the early fish lived in was dirty. Dirty water does not have much oxygen. So over millions of years these fish grew lungs as well as gills. This was so that they could breathe air from above the water. These fish are called lobe fins and they were able to breathe in or out of water.

About 350 million years ago the lobe fins began to drag themselves out of the water and onto the banks

Millions of years ago the lobe fins crawled from dried-up ponds to ones that were filled with water. On land they probably fed on insects living among the plants.

of the rivers. Here they probably fed on the huge numbers of insects that swarmed among the plants. The weather was growing hotter and many rivers and ponds were drying up. For a long time lobe fins had used their fins to move on the bottom of ponds. Now all those lobe fins that could not crawl from their dried-up pond to one filled with water died. Only those with the kind of fins that enabled them to crawl to another supply of water stayed alive.

So fins became more and more like legs. Animals were evolving. The lobe fins became the first animals with backbones to move on land.

Above: A fossil fern.

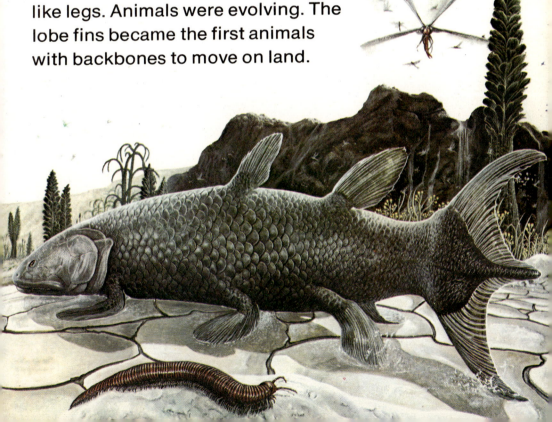

5 IN AND OUT OF WATER

An amphibian is an animal that can live in water and on land. As we have seen, the lobe fins could not stay out of the water for long. They were not true amphibians. But from the lobe fins came the first amphibians.

These first amphibians were the ichthyostegids. They looked much like lobe fins. But there were important differences. They had four legs, and each leg had five toes.

But these legs were not very

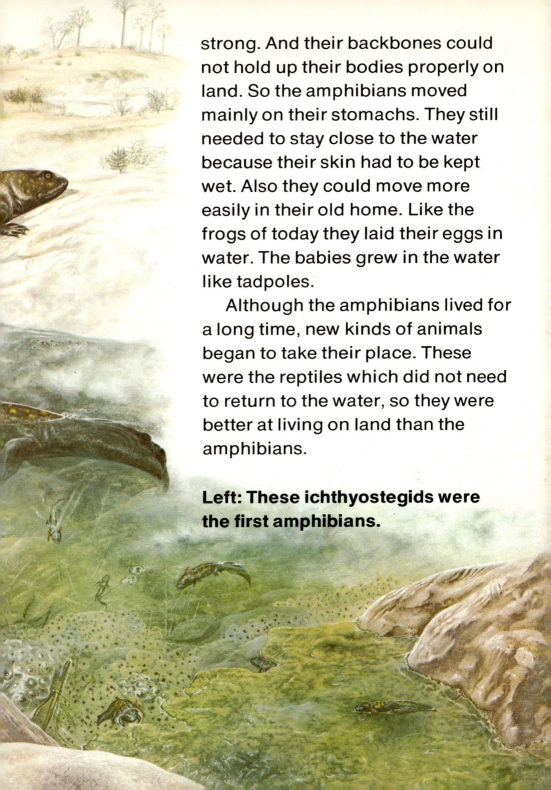

strong. And their backbones could not hold up their bodies properly on land. So the amphibians moved mainly on their stomachs. They still needed to stay close to the water because their skin had to be kept wet. Also they could move more easily in their old home. Like the frogs of today they laid their eggs in water. The babies grew in the water like tadpoles.

Although the amphibians lived for a long time, new kinds of animals began to take their place. These were the reptiles which did not need to return to the water, so they were better at living on land than the amphibians.

Left: These ichthyostegids were the first amphibians.

Above: Fossil eggs laid by a reptile of prehistoric times.

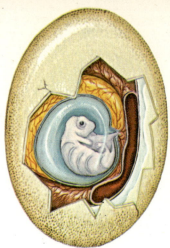

Above: Inside the hard shell the baby reptile grows safely.

6   FIRST REPTILES

The first reptiles looked much like the amphibians. But unlike them, the reptiles laid eggs with a hard shell. Inside the egg the baby could grow safely. When its body was strong enough the egg hatched.

The first reptiles were little animals called captorhinomorphs. They walked on legs that came out from the sides of their bodies. This meant they could not move easily. Over millions of years many other reptiles appeared from these first reptiles. But they developed upright legs which supported their bodies so they could move easily. These reptiles were of many shapes and

sizes. They lived in different ways. Some of the reptiles ate fish, some meat and some plants.

For about 65 million years the world was ruled by a group of reptiles called synapsids. These were very important because many millions of years later they developed into the mammals of today. Before the synapsids disappeared another group of reptiles began to appear. These were the ancestors of the dinosaur.

Below: The first reptiles' legs sprouted from the sides of their bodies.

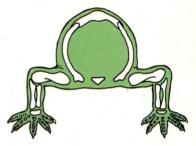

Below: Animals later developed upright legs.

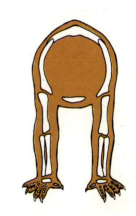

**Left:
1. Lystrosaurus was a plant-eating synapsid.
2. Hylonomus was a captorhinomorph.**

Above: 1. Euparkeria, the ancestor of the dinosaurs and of (2) Protosuchus.

7 TERRIBLE LIZARDS

The age of the dinosaurs began about 230 million years ago. It lasted for more than 150 million years. The word dinosaur comes from Greek words meaning 'terrible lizard'.

The ancestor of the dinosaurs was probably Euparkeria. This reptile walked on its back legs and used its short front legs for grasping. Euparkeria was also the

Crocodiles are relatives of the early reptile Protosuchus.

ancestor of crocodiles and birds.

Not long after Euparkeria, the first dinosaur appeared. There are two kinds of dinosaur. The difference between them is the way the bones of their hips were formed. One kind is the saurischian dinosaurs, and they had hip bones like lizards' hips. The other kind is the ornithiscian dinosaurs, and they had hip bones shaped like birds' hips.

Many of the dinosaurs were unbelievably huge. If you go to a museum you can see the skeletons that have been put together again.

Left: In some museums the bones of dinosaurs have been put together to make whole skeletons.

8 THE PLANT-EATERS

The plant-eating dinosaurs were the largest land animals ever to have lived. They are called sauropods and they were saurischian dinosaurs. They were descended from the Plateosaurus, one of the earliest dinosaurs. Plateosaurus was about six metres long and plodded about on all four legs. But as its back legs were larger than the front ones it could stand easily on its back legs.

One sauropod, called Camarasaurus, had front legs that were longer than its back ones. Like the other sauropods it was so heavy it walked on all fours. It used to be

Above: The sauropods were descended from Plateosaurus.

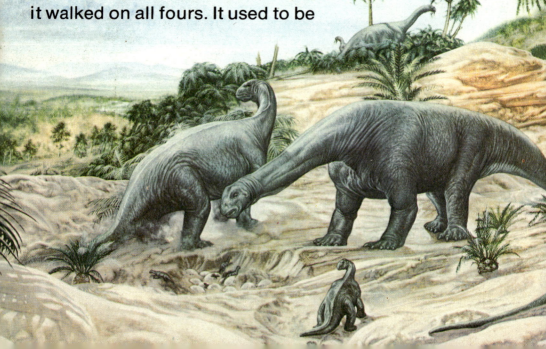

thought that the sauropods lived in water. But now scientists think that sauropods spent most of their lives on dry land. One reason is that their fairly narrow feet would have become stuck in the soft river mud.

These giants spent most of their time eating. Their very long, thin necks helped them to collect food. But their mouths were small and their teeth weak. So it took them a long time to eat all the food their great bodies needed.

Below: A group of Camarasaurus with their young. Like the other sauropods they spent most of their time feeding.

9 GENTLE GIANTS

The largest four-footed animal that ever lived was Brachiosaurus. It weighed 50 tonnes, nearly as much as two full grown elephants. It was 25 metres long. With its snake-like neck it stood more than twelve metres high. The Brachiosaurus spent most of its time on land where

Right: A fossil footprint of Cheirotheirum which was related to the ancestor of the sauropods, the largest four-footed animals that ever lived.

1

2

3

it fed on the leaves of tall trees rather like the elephants and giraffes of today. Diplodocus was even longer, though not so heavy. It was 30 metres from its head to its long tail.

Apatosaurus, the 'thunder lizard', was about 18 metres long. It had very thick legs. It left enormous footprints. But its tiny head was no heavier than one of its neck bones. It had no protecting armour. It could not defend itself nor attack others.

The plant-eating dinosaurs did not hurt other animals except by accident. They might tread on them or hit them with their tremendously heavy tails. But they had much to fear from the fierce meat-eating dinosaurs living at the same time.

Below: The size of (1) Brachiosaurus, (2) Diplodocus and (3) Apatosaurus shown against the size of a modern elephant and a Blue whale.

Waddling

Kicking and clawing

Crouching

Above: These are some of the movements of Tyrannosaurus.

10 THE MEAT-EATERS

The meat-eating dinosaurs were perhaps the most frightening animals that have ever lived. They are called theropods and were saurischian dinosaurs. The theropods ruled the forests and swamps. They terrified all other animals and ate the slow plant-eating sauropods. The theropods could run quickly on land but were fairly helpless in water.

The theropods were well armed. Their strong jaws and their front legs could tear great holes in other animals. Their front legs were not much use for anything else. The theropods usually walked on their

Sitting

Lying

back legs. They had short, heavy necks and long heads.

The largest and most terrifying dinosaur was Tyrannosaurus. It was the biggest of all meat-eaters. This fearful creature was 14 metres long and five metres high. It had teeth 15 centimetres long which could tear up the smaller dinosaurs quickly.

Not surprisingly the fierce theropods lasted much longer on Earth than the gentle sauropods.

Left: Tyrannosaurus was the largest meat-eater of all time.

11 BIRD-HIPPED DINOSAURS

The ornithoscia, or bird-hipped
dinosaurs, were all plant-eaters.
Many of these animals moved on all
four legs. But some of them, such as
Iguanodon, walked on two legs.
Iguanodon was the first dinosaur to
be discovered. It had very unusual
hands. Each hand had four long
fingers and a thumb shaped like a
large upright spike.

   The bird-hipped dinosaurs stayed

**Right: Stegosaurus used its spiky
tail to keep away its enemies.**

on Earth for longer than the giant sauropods. One reason was that many had good protection against their enemies. This was different kinds of strange bony plates on their skins. Stegosaurus had two rows of flat, bony plates running along the middle of its back. Along its tail were two pairs of bony spikes and it used its tail as a weapon.

Some of the last dinosaurs were the ceratopsians. They also had armour to protect them from their enemies. Protoceratops, for example, had a narrow, parrot-like beak, and a frill of bone like a collar.

Above: Iguanodons were plant-eating dinosaurs and lived together in herds.

Below: Protoceratops had a frill of bone to protect its head.

We have seen that life began in the sea and that gradually animals became able to live on land. Millions of years after leaving the water many animals went back to it, to escape from their enemies on land. Their legs and feet turned into flippers. Their tails grew into fins. They did not become fish. They stayed reptiles and breathed through lungs.

The plesiosaurs were a group of

Right: A long-necked plesiosaur reaches into the sky to catch a pterodactyl.

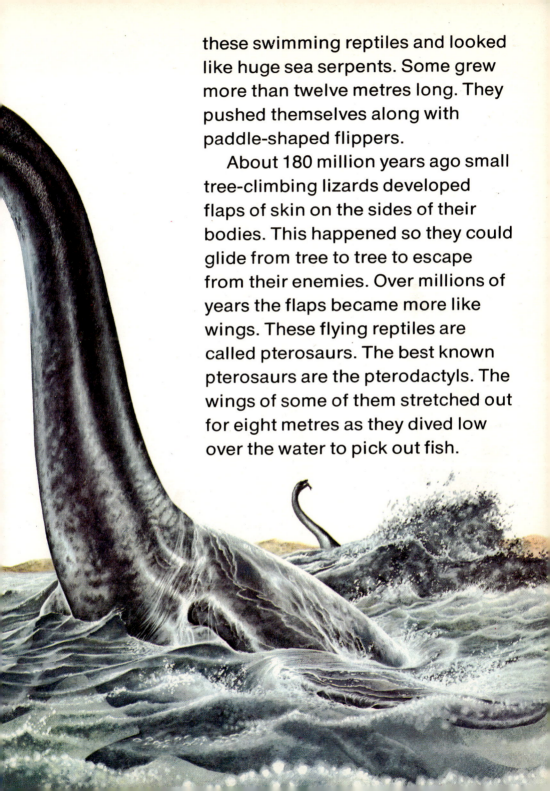

these swimming reptiles and looked like huge sea serpents. Some grew more than twelve metres long. They pushed themselves along with paddle-shaped flippers.

About 180 million years ago small tree-climbing lizards developed flaps of skin on the sides of their bodies. This happened so they could glide from tree to tree to escape from their enemies. Over millions of years the flaps became more like wings. These flying reptiles are called pterosaurs. The best known pterosaurs are the pterodactyls. The wings of some of them stretched out for eight metres as they dived low over the water to pick out fish.

About 70 million years ago a great many dinosaurs were still roaming the Earth. Then suddenly they seem to have disappeared, almost without warning. No dinosaur fossil is less than about 65 million years old. All reptiles died out except for lizards, crocodiles, snakes and turtles.

Why did this happen? Nobody knows for certain. But there were probably many reasons. There were

Right: All the dinosaurs have died out, leaving only modern reptiles.

Komodo Dragon

Snake

Tuatara

Crocodile

Tyrannosaurus Rex

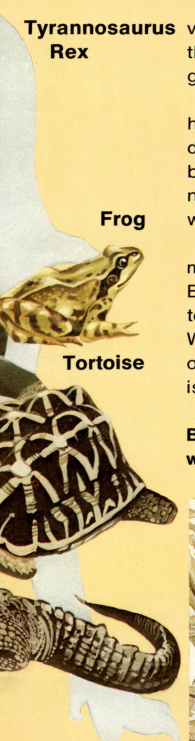

Frog

Tortoise

violent earthquakes at this time and there was no rain. This brought great changes to the Earth.

It may be that the Earth became hotter. Huge animals do not like hot days, especially if the weather becomes cold at night. But we do not know that such a change in the weather did happen.

Some people think that the mammals drove out the dinosaurs. But both kinds of animals had lived together for many millions of years. Why should one kind suddenly die out? Why the dinosaurs disappeared is still a mystery.

Below: These dinosaur bones show where a number of animals died.

Mammals are different from reptiles in many ways. They are warm-blooded. Their bodies are covered by hair and not by scales. Their babies grow in the mothers' bodies. Most of them are born and not hatched from eggs.

The earliest mammals lived about 200 million years ago. Most of them were quite small, about the size of rats. Horses, elephants, cats and dogs are some of the best known mammals today. Their ancestors lived in these early times.

Below: Eohippus was so small it would not have reached a horse's knees today.

The first kind of horse was Hyracotherium. It is better known as Eohippus, which means 'dawn horse'. It had four toes on the front feet and three toes on the back feet. It was no larger than a fox. Later came Mesohippus, or 'middle horse'. This had three toes and was the size of a large dog. The direct ancestor of our horse was the one-toed Pliohippus. Moeritherium was the ancestor of our elephant. It was about as big as a large pig. Miacis was the ancestor of our dog and cat and it looked like a weasel.

Above: The early mammals may have fed on the eggs of the dinosaurs.

Moeritherium was tiny compared with a modern elephant.

15 ICE AGE MAMMALS

About a million years ago ice began to creep down from the north. Much of Europe and North America turned into snowy wastes. Rivers of ice called glaciers formed all over the world. The Ice Age had arrived.

Many giant mammals lived at this time. Packs of giant wolves fed on the herds of bison which roamed the

Below: Smilodon, a North American sabre-toothed tiger, attacking a mastodon. Smilodon had two big fangs for tearing away the flesh of large animals.

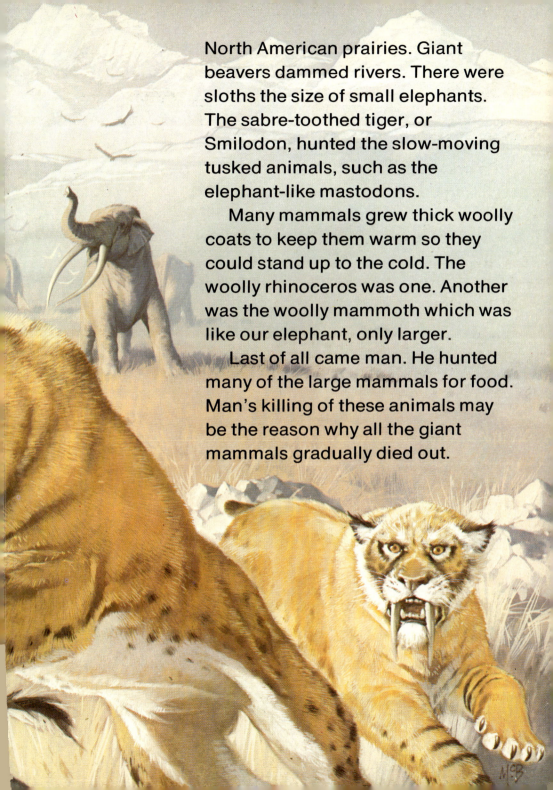

North American prairies. Giant beavers dammed rivers. There were sloths the size of small elephants. The sabre-toothed tiger, or Smilodon, hunted the slow-moving tusked animals, such as the elephant-like mastodons.

Many mammals grew thick woolly coats to keep them warm so they could stand up to the cold. The woolly rhinoceros was one. Another was the woolly mammoth which was like our elephant, only larger.

Last of all came man. He hunted many of the large mammals for food. Man's killing of these animals may be the reason why all the giant mammals gradually died out.

WORDS YOU MAY NOT KNOW

Ancestor   Someone or something that lived a long time ago and whose relationship to a present person can be directly traced through generations.

Enemy   Someone or something that is against another person or animal.

Evolution   The process by which simple kinds of animals and plants change over millions of years into more complex forms.

Gills   Organs of a fish or other water animal used for breathing underwater.

Laboratory   Room or building where scientists conduct their experiments.

Mammal   A warm-blooded creature which has a backbone.

Museum   A building where all sorts of interesting objects are on show and stored.

Nostril   One of the outside openings of the nose.

Prairie   Vast, flat grassland.

Scale   Horny overlapping plates.

Scientist   A person who studies science, such as chemistry, physics or biology.

Skeleton   The framework of bones which supports the body.

Swamp   Low-lying land filled with water.